WEB DESIGNER

© 2024 Julie Dascoli

All rights reserved. No part of this book may be reproduced or transmitted in any form or by any means, electronic or mechanical, including photocopying, recording or by any information storage and retrieval system, without prior permission in writing from the publisher.

Published in 2024 by Amba Press, Melbourne, Australia.
www.ambapress.com.au

Previously published in 2015 by Hawker Brownlow Education.
This edition replaces all previous editions.

ISBN: 9781923116962 (pbk)
ISBN: 9781923116979 (ebk)

A catalogue record for this book is available from the National Library of Australia.

WEB DESIGNER

Written by Julie Dascoli

Photography by Laura Dascoli

Dear Reader,

Welcome to this volume of the *Real People Real Careers* series. I hope you'll enjoy learning all about Nick and his work as a web designer.

Before you read on, I'd like to say a few thank-yous to the people who helped to make this book possible.

Firstly, thank you to Laura Dascoli, who took the photographs you see in the book, and to Donna Dascoli, who provided initial editing and computer support services.

Secondly, my thanks to the staff and students in Years 4, 5 and 6 of the Mossgiel Park Primary School class of 2015 for their unwavering help and support.

And finally, I'm grateful to Nick himself, who generously gave up his time to help others learn about his profession – and to show them all the ways in which his job rules!

Happy reading!

Julie Dascoli

WEB DESIGNER

A **web designer** is a person who is employed by businesses to design, build and manage their **websites**.

My name is Nick and this is the story of how I became a **web designer**.

I attended a private grammar school near my home. I worked as hard as I could at school and enjoyed all types of computer subjects. I loved to play computer games at home, too, but only once my homework was done.

In Year 9, I joined a **school exchange program** and was given the opportunity to go to Belgium, a country in Europe.

They speak the **French** language in this region, so I was able to practise the **French** that I had been learning and enjoying at school. It was very exciting and extremely educational.

I stayed with a family who had a son my age, and I did everything that their son did. I attended his classes and participated in the same sports that he did, just like a member of his family. I learned to speak **French** really well, and I have very fond memories of my exchange year.

The next year, I went back to the real world and normal Year 10. That year flew by, and before I knew it I was in Year 11. In Years 11 and 12, I did subjects like **multimedia**, maths, English, **French** and **information technology (IT)**. By this time, I thought I knew what I wanted to do, and I applied for a three-year **degree** in film and television production the following year. I was very happy when I discovered that I had a position in the course I wanted. While I was at **university**, I got a job as a **waiter** at a bar, as I needed money to run my car, get myself to and from **university** and go out occasionally with my friends.

The course was interesting, but I couldn't think of a job that I wanted to do in the film and television field. I was worried that I had wasted my time, but today I really believe that no education is a waste. I feel that I learned a lot of things during my first **qualification**, such as how to communicate effectively, the importance of self-confidence, and many other valuable skills that I have taken into the next phase of my career journey.

During my second year at **university**, friends and family started asking me to do computer jobs for them, such as giving advice about computers, building **websites** and providing **technical support**. I really liked this kind of work, and I decided that I wanted to do it as a career. I finished my **degree** and began looking for another course, this time in **IT**. After doing a lot of research and seeking the advice of my parents and teachers, I chose a **degree** in computer science.

> After doing a lot of research and seeking the advice of my parents and teachers, I chose a degree in computer science.

In the meantime, I saw a position advertised for a part-time **technical support** worker at a very well-known global computer company. I wondered if I could do this work and do a second **university degree** as well. Soon after the interview at the computer company, I received a phone call to say that I could start straight away and that they would schedule my hours to fit in with **university**. I was on my way!

I continued to work and go to **university** for some years while also doing a lot of private jobs at home. Eventually, I felt that it was time to leave the computer company and begin working for myself.

I am still at **university** doing computer science and loving it, as it's very relevant to my job. Meanwhile, my web design work is getting busier every day.

Tasks I perform every day

- → First, I check my emails, as this is where a lot of the communication with my clients occurs.

- → After checking my emails, I check my business social media accounts.

- → My day is then spent working through the tasks on my daily 'to do' list.

- → I make phone calls to clients and ask questions to make sure the work I do is exactly what they require.

- → In order to receive payment for my work, I need to check and send invoices.

- → I back up my data every second day.

- → In addition to my work from home, I go to **university** for 20 hours a week and complete any homework that my teachers have set for me.

Interesting facts about my job

- → I work about 15 hours per week on my web business.
- → I'm at **university** for 20 hours per week.
- → I allow about 15 hours per week to complete **university** assignments and related tasks.
- → I take short lunchbreaks whenever I can fit them in, which depends on what I am doing.
- → I currently have five clients.
- → My favourite task is seeing what I have created and receiving feedback.
- → My least favourite task is telling people how much the work I have done will cost them.

"I choose very comfortable clothes and shoes, since I do a lot of sitting"

What I wear to work

As I work alone in my office, I don't have to wear any sort of special uniform or dress code. I choose very comfortable clothes and shoes, since I do a lot of sitting.

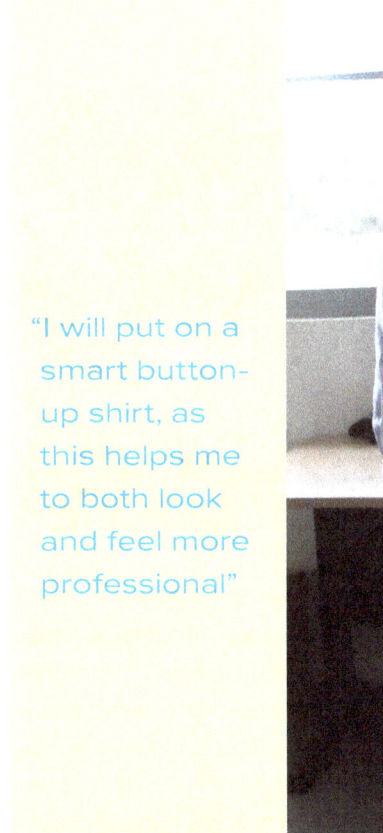

"I will put on a smart button-up shirt, as this helps me to both look and feel more professional"

When I am meeting with clients, however, I will put on a smart button-up shirt, as this helps me to both look and feel more professional.

In order to do my job, I need certain types of **equipment**. Firstly, I need an office and a fairly large desk along with an **ergonomic chair**. I also have both landline and mobile phones. I use two computers. One is a desktop for when I work at my desk, as the large screen makes it easier to do the work. I also have a laptop, which is portable, so I can take to it a meeting or work while I'm on holiday. I need a notebook to scribble down notes and a stencil to help me visualise shapes for the web pages.

> I need an office and a fairly large desk along with an ergonomic chair.

mathomat stencil

assorted pens

tablet

graph paper

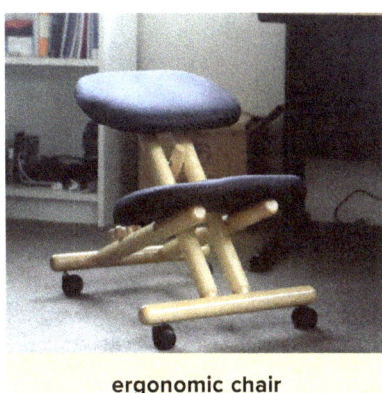
ergonomic chair

desk

WEB DESIGNER

What you need to do my job

- → You enjoy working indoors.
- → You enjoy talking to people.
- → You are good at using – or interested in learning how to use – a computer.
- → You enjoy helping others and their businesses.
- → You have plenty of **self-motivation**.

Related occupations

- → computer technician
- → computer salesperson
- → graphic designer
- → **technical support** worker (on-site or via the phone)
- → software designer

Postscript

Nick is currently working for himself as a **web designer**. He hopes to build up his business over time through advertising, word-of-mouth and plain hard work!

> You are good at using —
> or interested in learning how to use —
> a computer.

Glossary

Degree A **qualification** obtained at **university** upon completion of a course. *Nick completed a degree in film and television production but was not happy with the choice of jobs available with that* qualification.

Ergonomic chair A chair designed for office workers to help prevent back problems. *To do his work effectively, Nick needs an* **ergonomic chair**.

Equipment The tools that a person needs in order to do their job. *Nick uses a variety of* equipment, *including landline and mobile phones as well as a desktop computer and a laptop.*

French The national language of France. **French** is also spoken in other countries, including Belgium, Canada and many more. *Nick was able to practise the* French *he was already learning when he lived in Belgium for a year.*

Information technology (IT) Anything related to computers, including software, hardware and the internet. *Nick realised that what he really wanted was to pursue a career in* information technology (IT).

Multimedia The study of how several types of media can combine to communicate a message. Potential mediums include text, graphics, audio and video. *At high school,* **multimedia** *was one of Nick's subjects.*

Qualification The certificate, diploma or **degree** that proves you have completed training in a particular field. *Nick's first* qualification *was in film and television production.*

Self-motivation The ability to undertake a task or activity without another's supervision. *To become a web designer like Nick, you need to have good* self-motivation.

School exchange program A program that gives high school students the opportunity to live and study in another country. *Nick studied in Belgium for one year as part of a* school exchange program.

Technical support The act of giving support and advice to help customers to get the most from their mobile phones, computers and other technologies. *Nick was a* technical support *worker before he decided to work for himself instead.*

University A tertiary education facility where students can obtain a **degree**. *Nick is at* university *again to do his second* degree *in computer science.*

Waiter The employee at a restaurant who takes your order and brings your food and drinks. *Nick took a job as a* waiter *to earn some money while he was at* university.

Web designer A person who creates web pages on behalf of businesses that customers can access through the internet. *Nick is working for himself as a* web designer.

Website A set of interconnected web pages, usually created for the purpose of promotion or for sharing information. *Nick's current job involves building* websites *for businesses.*

return n.each
function(){return
var b=[["resolve"
function(){return
.fail(c.reject
.disable,b
function(a,b,c)
fail(g.reject)
n.readyWait
"onreadystatechange",
EventListener("DOMContent
setTimeout(f,50)}J()
"div"),e.style
c.removeChild
data(a,b,c)}else
if
void 0
in
"embed ":!0,"object
function
camelCase(d.slice(5
removeData(this
function(){n.dequeue
_removeData(a,
dequeue(this

Other titles in this series

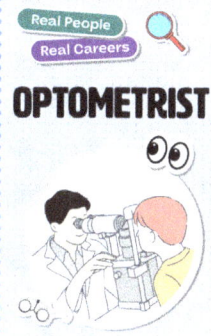

WEB DESIGNER PAGE 19

www.ingramcontent.com/pod-product-compliance
Lightning Source LLC
Chambersburg PA
CBHW052211110526
44591CB00012B/2164